ECHO
BAY

Jennifer Battisti

—
Tolsun Books
Tolleson, Arizona

for my mother

Contents

Lee Canyon, New Year's Day

Up a ways, the snow shields the barren like an immaculate lie,
suspends our questions for an hour.
We do not have to navigate our lives
here in this tiny globe.

Our daughter leaves wings in the frost,
eats balled up snow,
not yet knowing how short winter will be.
Our inevitable words sleep under heaps of clean white.

We will leave,
this marriage we made
like rows of orphaned snowmen we count
on our way down the mountain.

Each spectacular sphere we packed and heaved into love.
Our mittens soaked through.
Eyes thumb-deep, pine needle mouth,
the hat we sacrificed to make it believable.

The horizon thaws out our course
as we descend—
The blues, crisp, draping an impartial desert below.
And then, just vapor.

Later, the scent of the shower after they've gone,
a memory complete,
but without anywhere to point to
as if to say, we were here.

Tables Turned

Down where the showgirls sunbathed
on rooftops like a dozen golden swans—
their frothy feathered tails floating on dewy stages twice a night
was a studio apartment off N. 11th, my family's first dream,
the city still naked in 77.
Two pillows fixed to my small soft head, then bloomed,
Lucy in the sky.
An injection, a texture,
a genetic code set to a rhythm as known as my mother's heavy eyes.
Leaning slant on shag, stacked scripture beside the Technics player,
Sgt. Pepper's waiting, mustachioed,
in their Day-Glo military suits for me
to run my palm along the fuchsia flowers
that spelled out *Beatles*.
And now, 11th St. Records keeps walls of our stored memories,
each sleeve, slipped cover, contains
the capsule where the music carried us forward.
The fine needle in my lonely heart,
a delicate compass.
When pierced flush against the grooves, tables turned
I can go back.

Kitchen Sponge

She wonders how evolution
holds inside itself
a private extinction;
her synthetic skin hardening
on countertops
until she swallows suds to
suck up the mess of
domestication.
Her Porifera ancestors,
unapologetically lime green.
Slender stove pipe cylinders,
filtering the unseen alchemy of this planet.
The Venus Flower Baskets

enslaving shrimp with household chores.
She waits, porous and bitter,
outside the family basin,
the blue Brillo on her back,
a fiber nest of her fury
to scour out the marks—
her own choices, the only ones
she cannot abrade,
while longing to belong
to only the deep
wilderness of autonomy.

Fishing at Midnight

Night crouched in the cove like a beaten bird.
We set out our map—
            lake whiskey and a hand radio.

Over my mother's skinny legs,
a bonfire spilled shadows,

apparitions from an underworld
while she danced in the sand

to Madonna with my teenage sister.

            Ashes floated
in flashes of fire
softening them into children.

The new choreography—

release
from the fixed lure in our throats.

From the tent I'd made of lawn chair I could stand it—
watch my family's

bent faces,
suck on my own wet hair—feed the fleeting echoes
my grotesque fears.

I didn't see my father strip naked and
                        push off
angling sideways in his speedboat,
            drifting   into the darkness—

his fishing pole doubled over with a clean hook.

Every star hung its head.

        The moon hovered
over us, cracked in places

like shattered dishes glued back together,
refusing defeat.

The kind of loyalty I understood.

Off Boulder Highway

The hose water stung young lips,
a hot plastic surge into our mouths.
Later, we'd take heavy swallows off a 40 oz
the same way—until there was no space left to take in air.
The electric boxes were brownstone stoops,
only with reproductive repercussions.
What did we know—our asses burning each night
on the green alter of our adolescence.

If the Cuban boys liked you
they'd feed you fatty pork ribs you'd eat with both hands,
scoop bathtub jungle-juice into red solo cups two at a time.
They'd tag your name in block letters
on block walls with flames rising off the top,
like the force that could take you out of the neighborhood.

The nearby power plant umbrellaed us, a galvanic nanny
zipping, cracking, and humming an electric lullaby,
but the houses were no bigger than a tight fist.
Ceilings low enough to catch flung whiskey
leaving a stain, an ink blot I'd confuse with love.

My sister was the queen of the radio station—
requested Def Leopard all summer long
while tanning on the front lawn in chairs
that opened like love notes slipped in lockers.
Hysteria like a compass bearing,
Eastside our true north.

We'd circle the same zip code like chained dogs,
get 86'd from Nevada Palace
just to get our Polaroid on the casino wall,
cross streets that crossed our names off every list—

our roots growing like ash cylinders
on GPC cigarettes.

At Christmas we'd hang tinsel on real trees
bought from the carnies in desert lots,
tobacco dip fringing their grainy tongues.
They'd give discounts
on the ones with dead patches.
At night we'd build fires at Frenchman's mountain,
french kiss until we could no longer remember our address.
We'd look down on the city, the strip, a line
I'd snort up my nose for a decade straight.

When we ran out of pot we'd hyperventilate on purpose
then press palms on each other's ribs until the black gauze
wrapped us in absolute quiet,
until there was no space left to take in air.
The slump, then seize, a proof
of our residence inside our own bodies.

The God of Small Deaths

I prayed for the absence of shedding.
No red sparrows beneath my breath.
A zygote to fill my empty bowl.
Love's primitive absolute: to be kept.

I watched the doves at breakfast.
Their throats vibrated while I ate my crumbs.
Ivy climbed my uterine walls.
Flushed my breasts with the female song.

I checked and re-checked the felt tip sticks,
my ensuing milk ducts, the intranet.
I joined women in space.
The obsessive pit of reproduction chatter.

Then came the daily disclosures of sweet invasion.
I left spoonfuls of sesame on the feeder
while I added up how many weeks
I'd been a part of this universe.

Embryo enchantment,
I sank right down into my own yolk sac of ecstasy,
curled my toes into the alluring soil.
I had become unabbreviated.

The darker dove quick mounted and flapped
upon the lighter one, then fled just as fast.
I began to leak fuchsia,
doubled over with a fist fastened around my hope.

The viewing and wake made private
for mother and child.
I contracted inside and spat out loud.
My body diminished.

Seems absurd to mourn the passing of a grain of rice,
Fish spine, trout tail.
I bled out quick, the god of small deaths held my palm
while my cervix swelled with each passing possibility.

Repossession of the heavy heat,
the secret solace, pungent smells,
bits of earth,
the continent I had become.

I waited for a doctor to tell me what I already knew.
My mother folded and re-folded my clothes
into a neat stack while I soaked through the blue blanket,
and was sent home to become someone I had already buried.

The doves kept coming like sewer rats; I shunned them.
Two weeks later, I returned to my hollow diagnosis,
a haunting Hemorrhage,
to find it had clung like a snail to my insides.

Wheeled in, my gray face nodded
and handed over my fig leaf for blue socks,
bottoms rubber coated,
for traction.

The midnight nurses smiled in the female way,
took snapshots of the inky spot, a black hole draining a planet.
They pumped me full of strange blood
until the edges of the morning returned.

Placed upon the scissor bed,
the men whistled while a child cried down the hall.
I drank the good gas and a cactus burst in my throat.
They polished the blade and scraped me like a pumpkin.

Later, I left with the lie
of lingering hormones—running water after
the tornado ripped the bones
from the home.

Mirage

We may never know what caused it—
I told you, while you achieved the out-of-body
experience you always wanted;
heaved in and out of the dark hat of consciousness.

The morning after the attack,
the immaculate bed held your diminished form,
a vacancy I tried to match.
The antiseptic army sterilized intimacy,
removing traces of the father I knew like tarnish from steel.
Denial, a silk scarf swaddling me when I could not believe my own eyes.
The tiger could have been triggered—I told you.
The enchantment of a beehive hairdo,
or a group of anti-gay terrorists,
or illusion itself
millions of years of evolution which even love could not domesticate.

Aglow in the felt spun canyon
every window sealed shut
full of faces fat with thirst looking down into the gulch.
We all felt the incision—
the grip of the mandible.
Glory going dark that night.
The Kind Magician, sawed in half,
thirty teeth sharper than possession.
Bone, sinew, jaw, the sagittal crest blooming with darwinian truth,
as the show tiger drug him across the stage,
in a different brand of pageantry.

Every seat in the house
held this trick forever in their sight.
The secret tables held for the Casino Kings
and the sunken front row where
the elephant might piss before she disappears before your very eyes.

Your tower kept us on the edge of our seats.
Sun bleached bricks
and a view of the mortuary.
White Coats, the color of mercy,
ushered in the tubes and dials,
while I assured you I'd received a solid severance
after the audience wiped out the inventory
of stuffed striped tigers.

The velvet ropes were put away.
The marquee came down;
contortion, the new hot ticket in town.
Thirteen days later, sleight of hand, and you died.
Maybe levitation is a form of forgiveness, I hoped.
Everything has its finale, my Father, my Headliner.
Montecore, the savage show tiger with the blue-gray
eyes outlived you,
proved Power and Speculation,
the trap doors of the heart,
just smoke and mirrors.

The First Week

The white orchids came two days before you did.
Balled up into four milky fists, they hung from the green branch
suspended like a primitive solitude.

The first bloomed while we were at the hospital;
its quiet rupture split stalks into a fit of pearly limbs.
The gummy petals arched out saluting your homecoming.

I latched and re-latched your searching mouth to my clumsy breast.
And as the night curled up and spooned the awaiting dawn
another sprout shot open while you slept upon my weepy chest
like a teacup on its saucer.

Engorged with milk and fear, I offered my bosom like a ham sandwich;
spun you around into the many different positions the book illustrated.
The last two buds held tight in their clammy homes refusing, it seemed,
to budge.

I lathered on the nipple balm and cursed the hippies
who had said this would come naturally.
In the quietest part of the night, sleep and hope had left
like dejected houseguests.
The largest flower unfurled,

first like a claw, then by morning into a silky kiss on a vine.
I brought you to bed with me, our skin bare, our breathing unanimous.
I slept for the first time,

woke to find you nursing as if we were old pros.
I felt the deep pull of motherhood.
The glorious becoming by a ferocious undoing.

By sunrise the last bloom had opened
and was reclining toward the window,
and the first bud already shedding gauzy petals
onto the table.

Off Duty Elvis

Early morning dust and neon
made fragile by the sun.
The grit and smut orphaned
by the goblins of the night.

By noon, the writers conference
will have me tucked
firmly in its palm.
Wearing doubt like a well-fitting garment,
I check my boarding pass: D gates.
The Vegas airport carpet bursts
into pattered blooms of fuchsia, canary;
a seamless swirling hypnosis pulling me
toward the shuttle.

Outside the gates,
a carousel of slot machines lurch like bullies
waiting to steal lunch money
and double knotted dreams.
I consider the absurdity of my pursuit.

And then, there he was, a mere few feet away—Elvis,
mowing down a Croissan'wich.
The King was eating at Burger King.
He was having it his way;
with coffee and hash brown disks.
His sideburns were perfect—
greasy minnows suctioned along his jaw.
The shimmer of rose oil and Vaseline beneath
the fluorescent lights left
Presley haloed in the luminous sheen.

The croissant flaked crumb by crumb onto the table
like single roses or undies from vulgar women.

He wore running shoes.
Plain white Reeboks—
His blue suede tucked in his carry-on, perhaps.

Sadly, he was the bloated seasoned Elvis.
And, I suspect, on his way out of the impersonation biz.
A final Heartbreak Hotel for this middle-aged charade.
Then, suddenly, he looked up to check the flight information.
The resemblance was unmistakable.
Those tender, soulful eyes.
This was a costume he never questioned,
nor removed.
Swallowed up into the belly of the bird, I suctioned pen to paper.
Going where I need to go,
to chase the fever which never relents—
That gyration inside my heart.

Jackalope

The root was always buried in the burrow of my womb
dilating like a fireside cowboy tale,
thicker with each re-telling
I pushed my body into two—
a downy-fleshed baby
detonated whole hunks of my anatomy.
A taxidermy into motherhood,
this new arrangement of skin, strange
and ugly.

The sharp tips first pierced fur,
blood pooling in the spots where
I had to break, then
suddenly—antlers!
Seized embers extended on my crown.
A bulky cage I raged against.
The matted holes sodden and
sutured with breast milk and baby wipes.

Agility, a lullaby I cooed into
doughy fists reaching.
My hindquarters clenched,
set to spring at sudden fever
or when the unremarkable tedium
nursed at my sanity.

Like my life, my antlers steadied:
A tumbleweed breached mid-flight.
I hung onesies on each peak to dry,
kept cooled cabbage leaves ready for engorgment.
Precision wrung me out each night.

Eyes burned pink visions of dangers
which before were black.

Unless my baby curled in the saucers
of my immense ears, I could not relax.
The veins, like blue bassinets lacing mythical stories

from postcards in ghost towns I'd left behind.
Most days I felt stuffed, replicated,
unlikely of this impossible creation.

Soon velvet dressed the bone like a love
I could not undo and I could no longer recall
the lightness of what was before.

The Resurrection

He loads the dishwasher, mindfully,
Stonehenge with an extra rinse cycle.
I chant: *road trip, date night,*
bury the spite below the worms—
airtight.

He bakes an abracadabra shepherd's pie
swollen with a hundred years of sorcery.
I pair socks, the curled fabric
and decisive elastic an intimacy I can hardly bear.
We paint our faces, the color of ancient pain:
yellow mica, gummy tar, full-bloom peacock,
which flecks like hunger under the full moon.
We draw a ring in the sand.
In the center we place our marriage—
a forgotten heap.

We whirl, stabbing at the plague,
trying to disenchant ourselves of ritual and fury.
We arch, reach skyward, smudged in a haze of sage,
We plead with the stars.
We dance. Teeth clenched around arrow-headed spears
we've promised to dull.
Our bodies swell, bend like illusion,
Wild, stark, flailing around the fire until our
muscles collapse against Institution.

We are tired. Belief, light as a feather, stiff as a board.
We circle the mass like giant grieving elephants,
poking at the dead thing with sticks. I examine the bones,
knowing the anatomy of torment by touch alone.
He weeps over the marooned remains,
nudging them for confirmation.
I cover it with feathers and photographs,

trinkets from its past. We spit at it together,
A blessing. Finally seeing mercy
is the greatest witchcraft of all.

Communion

I can feel my bones moving, Mommy—
They sound like drums,

she says, her four-year-old
body still dew damp like new sod,
not yet tethered to earth.
The evidence barely visible now
of the small animal which once curled in the crook
of my forearm like a fortune I had not earned.
The Truth dilates inside her,
ligaments stretch past
her need for me.
She will begin to see my inadequacy,
the flimsy thread running through my life.
On the floor, she squirms
in orthopedic bewilderment,
her skin eclipses a tectonic tantrum.
A growth spurt, shifting us—
her into the world of *choosing* her words.
Her inexhaustible spirit folded,
a tidy place to insert the ineffable size of childhood.
Her lady bug bib hung up, she is finally a slave to melatonin,
inside voices, and the shapeshifting gremlins of esteem—
will the preschoolers like her hair?
I inherit whole yards of empty-handed moments
without a cry to quiet.
A planet free of simple amniotic warmth.
My hips haunted by the phantom
baby straddling the notion of being separate.
I remember our placenta, our first Communion,
brought home with us in the red cooler
for the doula to dehydrate into immunity
against the postpartum apparitions.
Bizarre in my kitchen beside the coffeepot,

an organ grown and expelled in under a year
suddenly juxtaposed into this place where I toast bread.
Her gloved hands pointed to arteries leading to our past life.
The cord binding our two dimensions,
soup cans on a string,
is now a wound faded by Time.
I tell my daughter her bones are becoming hard
she'll be strong against the world—
I scoop her lean form into my arms, the soft spot
closely between us.

St. Augustine Beach

—FL, our nation's oldest city

When my father saw her sunbathing
her lean body that would one day
push me from it, over and over,
maybe he knew in an instant
his bohemian life had ended.

Knew from the string-tied birds
fastened around her figure,
her wide hands, two starfish holding
Helter Skelter, sand in the creases.
Perhaps the tide opened him,
deep in that place that would later shut down
just before my ninth birthday.

My mother bloomed like plankton and saw
her whole future hanging on his hanker-chief stick.
The way she would one day rest on his back,
and be carried away from her own soul.

He might have tossed his black hair just right
to catch the sunlight and smile the way I remember—
super nova.
She may have mistaken him
with the indigo depth in the quiet distance
and agreed to a date.

Later that week her nerves spilled food on him.
A waterfront seafood place anchored
with rusted steel and barnacles.
Her oval tray and narrow arms never large enough.
A decade later he would spill food on himself,
nightly anchored by a furrowed brow and fermented silence.

Maybe when he walked down that beach
searching for seagulls and sunsets,
he could have considered
the many invertebrates beneath his feet,
the ones not yet to shore.
The krill swarm he would leave behind
when the dividing tide came to swallow him up.

Instead they drove off.
The backseat filled with my father's
bow and arrows, a deck of cards
those things that would take up all the space.

My mother without bones
folded like a jellyfish to his side.
Waiting, as we all would,
for the humpback's song—
for another lagoon.

View from Lone Mountain

The Strip glints, pennies winking.
Each flipped wish
sunken into the black vast
desert we cannot see
but feel is here.
The Mojave cradles
this strange cup of longings in her center—
a child who fits and kicks,
fights sleep.
Nurses the colic away with lavender sunrises
dipped in coyote's breath.

The Exhibit

The neighbors crane out of their doorways
little children held flush to their sides.
I am the Grim Reaper of matrimony,
as if ambulance, or hearse,
proof of the worst kind—
something you made can stop breathing,
bleed beyond repair.

A stampede of repercussions barrels down the block,
the U-Haul groaning into our driveway.
An unearthed mammoth mascot
on the driver's side—
twin tusks jutting towards our front door
guarding second thoughts, cold feet.

The loading ramp swallows the evidence,
an aisle taking one half, a perforation—
splitting as simple as a paper towel torn
down the middle.
Our wooly dreams cocooned in old newspaper.

Our marriage sails away,
without procession.
Love now measured in feet,
owing only the mileage it stole.
The fossil of us mired in the swamp,
for me to carry
inside the storage unit of my body.

Later, when I tell the wives on the block
that our love was an endangered species
long before it went extinct,
they clench their jaws
while cutting back rosemary stalks escaping
from their clean, neat rows.

Terra Firma

My mother told me the story again after the surgeon took
the tangerine-sized tumor from her liver
in the same hospital where I came from her body
four decades earlier.
The story—which made it this far—
feels like a beige velour couch, the mechanism of a rotary phone,
sounds like a record flush against the soft rubber on the turn table.

In the summer of 1974 halfway through Texas,
my father insisted my mother drive while he slept,
to wake him in El Paso.
The journey—a line I can trace with my finger
but not with my memory: Florida to Las Vegas.
A big blind.
The Chevy Vega held my father's notebook,
his findings on bio-rhythms and their effect
on poker games and his new family.
My mother, hung like a fern over her hopeful future
and her four-year-old daughter sleeping in the backseat.

The first time I heard the story I was nine,
and had never heard the word *Abduction.*
It was as if all the mysteries of the world were solved
with that one word placed bare on my tongue.
I pictured Drew Barrymore in E.T.
I wondered if I left a trail of Reese's Pieces,
if I could catapult myself back in time, before I was born,
and clutch my mother's leg
at the only gas station for miles, in Mexico, where they were returned.
The store clerk pointing to Juarez on the map,
shouting *aqui! aqui!*

I imagine, standing with my sister witnessing
our parents become scavengers
for the five hours and 18-foot wall they somehow evaded,

without recollection.
I would feel the embarrassment—feel it again years later
when my mom had an address wrong,
could have sworn the movie started at 3,
or told us that our father was just *exhausted*.

Mother apologizing to everyone,
even the gas station attendant,
explaining it was a mystery—*misterio*.
They were there on the highway,
and then here on this dirt road—*perdido*,
the Spanish man concluded,
handing the map back to my father,
From then on, *lost*
was also, an inspection, a way to be probed,
a dark place for a specimen to be kept.

Later I searched my flesh for a marker—
Something that resembled the gray pearl
the dermatologist cut out of my father
after the strange spot kept weeping like a tide pool.
I wanted the kind of telepathy
which could explain the crisp-dead grass
flattened by crop circles in our living room.
My sister was anointed with a
a perfect spear in the center of her forehead.
A talisman. A locket containing the universe condensed.
Carrying forever the salve to bind us back together.

Juarez now claims hundreds of abductions, mostly women,
taken not by celestial beings but by other white lights in the night.
The estranged pearl, our extraterrestrial eavesdropper—
dropped into a sterile-metal bowl, flashed stardust—
reverberated love's malignancies,
and then was destroyed without our consent.

I would wonder all my life if *they* would come back for me.
Every time I set off an alarm at a security checkpoint,
or dreamt of the White Wheel which seized
gravity and magnetized my limbs,
I would secretly brace myself, hoping I'd finally been laced
with my family, to see into the Mothership, the beginning.
When the world was benign. To know how it felt
to be hovered upon, and then reconciled to solid earth.

Dead Weight

His leg that would dangle,
smooth and hairless
off the side of the couch like a limp vegetable,
owned all the silence in the room.
Polio became a word as sinful as stealing.

When secure in its brace, the cumbersome cage,
the tight rods were solid actors for joints,
the nuts and bolts imposters for ligaments.
We kept Legos far from his path—
for the impending fear of losing our balance.
The chill of the silver turned him into a secret man,
turned me into a careful bird as we all pivoted for affliction.

When free to shower, or on Sundays tucked
inside his robe,
the brace would lean in the far corner,
the small shoe still attached.
I wondered what wrong it had done to end up
in a place meant for punishment.

The smallest things chaffed at our skin.
My mother bought two sets of shoes, three sizes apart for him.
My sister handed out black eyes to wise mouth kids.
I followed him, mimicking his rhythmic limp,
trying to find a familiar stride.

But eventually, I understood—
a malady can attack its host,
leave abrasions and weeping
that only whiskey will cure.
And when the doctors said I was pigeon-toed,
was indeed a bird—
the corrective high-tops meant to mend the inversion
were flushed down his toilet.

Valley of Fire

The rocks unveil their beauty ignited,
the road slick with sun
spreads easily, like a woman
opening her inside parts.
Soft-shell, hot-core of her fiercest secrets.

Behind the blazing hills:
a haunting hologram of my father.
He casts his line—
The water's black center rises up.
Fish seek the same hurl
over and over; abandonment's warm hook.

Hostility hatches without warning—
My husband's face growing hard,
already eroding into my seat where I sit
stung by a dozen hysterical bees—
This discord is a twisted homesick trick.

My mother, an apparition, is buckled in beside me
in the passenger seat of my life.
Even as I try to unhinge, we are the same.
The strap locks, I choke. Restrained by history.
My grandmothers face wrought with fret,
my mother's absorbency, my daughter's fresh antenna
blooming in the backseat.

In each shadow rising off the backs
of the stone-faced Seven Sisters,
I am held up, kept from crawling
quick like a coward into the cool sand tunnels.

The petroglyphs rake their way out,
until truth is etched—
the five-limbed horned beast,

or a handprint of a prehistoric self.
As if abrading my own soul
could bring me back into the cave
where art and history are the same.

My life stands up from the atlas,
pulling curvy roads from its wrists
dusting off the Mojave from its legs,
stretching out its lean body along the interstate.

The red clawed feet, hollowed out cages rung with steps
where I climb out, feel my latitude like a steel rod in my spine.
I shed the snake, out of the solitary muscle,
grow into an Iguana, bearded by my past,
crown on my jaw,
and walk straight into the fire.

Barbie Gets a Second Chance

Well into the meat of her ninth year,
my stepdaughter decides to give Barbie a second chance.
Initiated, no doubt, by the budding enthusiasm of her 16-month-old sister,
and the alluring lineup of rubber toys on the lip of the bathtub:
the freckled frog who squirts water into an arc of tomfoolery,
the purple octopus with that mischievous smile,
a triplet of google-eyed tugboats.

Buried deep in the back of her closet
is a boneyard for Dora the Explorer, Tinkerbell,
Barbie and her imposters
shamed and swapped out for the mystical: flat irons, iPhones, fashion.
The tween gleam had catapulted the old standbys into toy purgatory,
until today.

My stepdaughter drops the dolls into the bath
two with ratted hair and a puzzling amputated third,
her single arm mechanically gesturing
that her missing pieces will not define her.
I suspect my stepdaughter waits for the spell of imagination to rise up.
But the dolls just pose, grinning beauty queens.

Barbie's arms reach out in desperation, but not a splash is made.
Their modern seams summon a flexible display
of frozen provocation—without the spark.
My stepdaughter breaks up
a second time. The figures float face down.
The polyvinyl pantomimes
abandoned altogether in one swift soggy move—
She sees their perfectly parted plastic lips
are speechless. The hardened magic,
lumps of leggy lies suspended and buoyant.

Life will keep spoiling the splendid,
chiseling the soft, the remarkable, into a predictable dullness.
She yanks the drain and towels off, already forgetting about invention
and the color of delight, letting childhood go, twice.

On Wondering What the Pig-Masked Men Were After the Night the Bellagio Rolex Store Was Nearly Burglarized

The sound of sledgehammers,
like winning at dawn,
the old Vegas way—
Back when surveillance had an accent,
jeweled elephants doubled down on blackjack,
and Evil Kinevil sailed over single-file sedans
like a sin-city slingshot.

Witnesses said it sounded like gunshots.
But I imagine it was more sensual, like
an abolished slot machine pouring
silver promise into a plastic bucket,
with an ad for all-you-can-eat on the side.

The shatter, the sound of remembering,
the way the scent of dirty coins is like a baptism.
Maybe that's all those piggies were after,
to free the time capsule—
their prom night at Alpine Village.
When taking a thing was possible.
The collective dismembering of molecules,
spidered the cool glass like a plague, and
was still for a moment before exploding
onto their slick tuxedos like Sammy Davis Jr.

These days, if you want to find Vegas,
you'll have to look closely,
past Minnie Mouse selfies on the strip
and the Little Darlin's annual Easter egg hunt.
You'll have to learn to teeter on edges, like big horn sheep
balancing the sun atop their keratin head dresses
like an aging showgirl, holding her breath,
waiting for the next quick change.

Echo Bay

In each flash of mile marker
my mind launches in reverse.
Tattooed on rusty cliffs,
a sun-bleached bereavement ring
unfolds like a paper map.

Divinity is the hem of assembly, I remember.
My ritual finger-nail half-moons etched on Styrofoam cups,
earth worms mining soil like segmented sacrifices.
In 1984 we'd insert our speedboat, a baptism,
the small salvation when everything
except physics failed us.

Today, drought exposes sunken sorrows,
small cities, the way I've anchored my
childhood to your shadow.
You are here, in each curve of prickly pear;
its stubble softening me as I head down the hill.

A hawk perches in half-submerged tire treads
buoyed only by longing—
My grief is a row boat in the desert
thundering nowhere,
waiting for a ghost.

A Great Blue Heron dives
from its aluminum siding nest,
rattling the marina's skeleton.
Wind barrels down the docks.
Somewhere, the giant catfish I feared laces whiskers
around the silver-minnow lures we sank
into the Black Canyon canals.

Boat slips, cracked in two, hardly
hold me now.

The weight of memory
splits seams like broken clam shells.
There are only bones, reverberations,
the indissoluble wake your death has made.
The shallow tide exhaling,
a haunting I've kept holding.

I want to believe more in alchemy than algorithms,
that ecology is more accurate than story.
Weeds burst out, reclaiming, remitting—
every empty space green.
Photosynthesis rises into the places
hollowed by loss, the places
we could not stay.

When No One is Looking

If you live long enough in Las Vegas
you will not learn to count cards.
You will learn to count triple-digit-days.
You will learn, this state is a broken tooth—
our city, the sharp tip
meant to shred inhibitions
into puréed pleasure.

While everyone else bolsters worth
in booths and bottles,
we have the best view
of her celebrity cerulean swirl
tangerine-silk carpet she unfurls
every day at dusk.

While heap of pedestrian—
one-moving-organism, glides across the Blvd
being transported, up escalator,
moving walkway, monorail, roulette,
cabana and cocaine—
our mountains howl, backed by wild burro
and barbed beavertail, above rows of bulldozers,
their raised shanks like scorpion.

From Calico Basin to Death Valley
We only wager on the desert—
on cacti-blooms, unhinged moonflowers
bursting at midnight. When no one is looking,
when everyone else is trying to find their way out
of the casino labyrinth
symphony of slots that sing *stay.*

The blossoms like white stars veiled in twilight dust
will be wilted by morning—

an implosion of the idea
that stacked-chips and swizzle-sticks
could ever bluff the Mojave.

The house, guarded by endless Joshua leaning in counsel,
always wins.

Gratitude & Acknowledgements

This chapbook belongs to her majesty, the Mojave, and to my daughter, Violet, whose fierce soul makes me a braver human. To my family and friends—Mom, Dad, Kim, Andrea, Laura, Maria, Britten, Anna, Brooke, Kian, Kenzie, Jayden—for their endless encouragement and support of my work. To the vibrant voices of the Las Vegas poetry community and their tireless efforts to cultivate a buffet of literary love for our city.

This book would not exist without the extraordinary mentorship of my dear friend, teacher, and editor, Heather Lang. My deepest appreciation for her guidance, insight, and attention to *Echo Bay*, and for her willingness to off-road in the name of poetry.

Many thanks to Timothy Lindner for all of the hard work and dedication.

Thank you to David Pischke, Brandi Pischke, and Tolsun Books for publishing *Echo Bay*.

Thank you to the editors of the publications in which versions of some of these poems have previously appeared: *Desert Companion; FLARE; Helen: A Literary Magazine; Legs of Tumbleweeds, Wings of Lace: An Anthology of Literature by Nevada Women;* and *Minerva Rising.*

Jennifer Battisti

Jennifer Battisti, a Las Vegas native, studied creative writing at the College of Southern Nevada. Her work has appeared in the anthology, *Legs of Tumbleweed, Wings of Lace*, and is forthcoming in *Where We Live*, an anthology of writing and art in response to the October 1st tragedy, as well as *The Desert Companion, Minerva Rising, The Citron Review, FLARE, Helen: A Literary magazine, The Red Rock Review, 300 Days of Summer* and elsewhere. In 2016 Nevada Public Radio interviewed her about her poetry. She holds a leadership position on the Las Vegas Poets Organization and is the administer and a participating teaching artist for the Alzheimer's Poetry Project in Nevada. This is her first chapbook.

16501043R00032

Made in the USA
Lexington, KY
16 November 2018